Old to New

Focus: Recycling

Meredith Costain

We used old things
to make new things.

We used plastic bottles
to make these masks.

We used plastic bottles
to make these hand puppets.

We used boxes and foil
to make this robot.

We used boxes and wheels
to make this tank.

We used an egg carton
to make this caterpillar.

We used an egg carton
to make this dinosaur.